HOW TO FIND OUT THE REAL PRICE OF RENTAL PROPERTIES?

BY

TAMI LAN

Copyright © 2019 by author.

All rights reserved.

No part of this book may be reproduced in any manner without written permission except in the case of brief quotations included in critical articles and reviews. For information, please contact the author.

TABLE OF CONTENTS

I.   Introduction   ...   1

II.   Chapter 1
Realtors / Brokers / Agents   ...   2

III.   Chapter 2
Seller   ...   4

IV.   Chapter 3
Mortgages   ...   9

V.   Chapter 4
Appreciation   ...   14

VI.   Chapter 5
Real Price of a Rental Property   ...   20

INTRODUCTION

If you are here, it means that you have already decided to make an investment in rental real estate. It could either be residential or commercial.

While my analysis will primarily use commercial property as a template, the approach to finding out the true value of a rental property is pretty straight forward and can be applied to residential properties, as well. But before we get to it, I just want to inform you about some of the aspects, factors and variables of real estate transactions that you should be aware of.

Because it is not enough to just know the answers. You need to know how they were derived.

Chapter 1

REALTORS / BROKERS / AGENTS

They are the first variable that you should be cautious about. It is standard practice for the seller's agent (also known as listing agent) to be paid a certain percentage of the sale consideration as remuneration (commission) for their efforts. This percentage is usually 5-7, although it be could more or less depending on multiple factors. If the buyer involves an agent, then the buyer's agent will be paid his dues from the listing agent's share of the commission. The sharing ratio is decided between the agents and it does not really make a difference to the investor.

Of course, the agents do mean you well but you should understand that their payout does depend on the price at which the sale concludes. In other words, the more expensive the property is sold/purchased, the more the agent(s) gets paid.

Inherently, there never really is any incentive for the agent/broker to be interested in the reduction of the list price.

Of course, one could mount the argument that the agent would be happy to see a sale happen for a lower price than no sale at all at a higher price. But that attitude may not settle in until the agent is in a desperate situation.

So, if you are out and about hustling to find the best listings out there, do not be surprised if you are out there by yourself and that no one else feels or understands the drive and passion that you have burning at the bottom of your belly.

Most importantly, do not be discouraged or beat-down even if you come across many agents that do not understand from where your offer comes from or arrogantly ridicule you. I am confident that in time, you will find your "Jerry Maguire". Just keep hustling and keep fighting the tides of ignorance.

Chapter 2

SELLER

This second variable is rather predictable. The seller is obviously trying to get the best or maximum price for the property. While that is not a wrong intention, it does become a deterrent to trade when the seller becomes greedy and overprices his property. I'm not talking about formal overpricing by 10-20% which get discounted eventually during the regular dance of negotiation. I'm talking about overpricing by a 100-110%. This is especially true in commercial real estate.

Most of you might be aware that every time you check the listings of commercial properties, a majority of them boast a 5-6% capitalization (cap) rate. Now, this cap rate is derived by dividing the rent that the property is currently generating by the list price.

$$\text{Cap Rate (\%)} = \frac{\text{Rent}}{\text{List Price}} \times 100$$

Example: (will use same figures throughout)

List Price = $1,800,000

Current Rent = $100,000

Cap Rate = (100,000 / 1,800,000) x 100

= 0.055 x 100

= 5.5%

So, when it comes to deciding on the list price, what happens almost every time is that the seller chooses a price that will reflect a cap rate of about 5-6%. The seller, his agent and even the market in general, might opine that this is a fantastic return on investment (ROI) and for the same reason, that the property is priced reasonably and that it is worth buying the property at the listed price.

Let me dismantle this point of view.

The symbol " ~ " shall mean 'approximately', 'around' or 'about'.

As of 2019, the banks offer as high as 2.5% interest annually for CDs (Certificate of Deposit) and 2% interest for savings account. The only other readily considerable choices of investments left are stocks & bonds, businesses and real estate. Before I proceed further, <u>let me just state it for the record that risk is involved in everything.</u> Even if you are just sitting at home, the roof can come crashing down on your head. You should know this by now. So, I hope I do not have to keep repeating this disclaimer every time that I discuss an avenue of investment.

Regarding stocks & bonds, any well-established wealth management company would claim that they anticipate ~ 4-7% return on investment in stock portfolios. Were this to be true, then why would anyone be interested in investing in real estate which projects a cap rate of only 5-6%? Especially when both the work and risk are higher in comparison to investing in stocks & bonds.

Businesses are at the other end of the spectrum. They embrace the highest form of risk but they also provide the chance to see the highest rates of return on investment. The cap rate could easily be 9, 12% or even 22, 36%. But if the business fails, the rate of return could be zero and in addition, the capital or principal could also be lost.

The truth of the matter is, real estate is meant to give a higher rate of return in comparison to stocks and bonds but not with the level of risk associated with running a business. Therefore, we can reasonably infer that no real estate investment is worth the effort, unless it provides a cap rate that is 9% or higher.

Now, if this theory of mine were to be true, then why is everyone on the real estate market advertising a cap rate of 5-6% as attractive? Well, for one reason, these would be acceptable investments to people who already have all the money they need to purchase the property (in other words, no mortgage) and is also looking for a way to hedge.

Hedging means committing investment to a cause that exposes it to lesser risks. When a person is dealing with a lot of liquidity (plain cash), hedging is done to almost certainly secure it from loss, even if it be at the cost of low or no returns, and especially to tackle issues like loss due to inflation of currency value or any other kinds of highly volatile or fluctuating market trends.

So, in that process of hedging, if you can get a better return on investment, compared to bank deposits or stock portfolios, isn't that the best deal ever? Yes, it is... *if...* you had all the money required to purchase that rental property all by yourself.

However, in addition to your out-of-pocket expenses, if you're looking to take out a loan/mortgage, especially for about 50-80% of the purchase price which would also include closing costs (we can approximately estimate it to 1 to 3% of the sale consideration), then the cap rate of 5-6% means absolutely nothing. Let me show you how.

Chapter 3

MORTGAGES

This is the aspect that buyers are most strained by and that sellers fail to consider. How many people in this country can afford to pay full price on purchase of property of even a few hundred thousand dollars, without using a loan/mortgage? Even the millionaires and billionaires; would they rather put all their money in one place? or would they split that money into ten parts and invest in ten properties, all of them supported by a mortgage but still producing cash flow?

So, even to rich people, it would make absolutely no sense to purchase a property that gives a cap rate of 5-6%, when they are to take out a loan/mortgage.

Why exactly does taking out a mortgage not work? Well, for starters, the current rate of interest on loans/mortgages used for investment in purchase of rental real estate is ~ 5%. When you amortize repayment of your loan amount for a period of 10 years, your monthly or yearly payment towards repaying that debt (also called debt service) which comprises of both the interest and the principal, works out to be ~12.7% <u>of the loan amount</u>.

List Price	$ 1,800,000.00		
Down Payment	$ 360,000.00	20%	
Loan Amount	$ 1,440,000.00	80%	
Mortgage Interest	5%		
Mortgage Period	10	years	
Monthly Payment	$ 15,273.43	Based on a preset calculation	
Yearly Payment	$ 183,281.21		
Repayment Rate	1.06%	Monthly	
Repayment Rate	12.73%	Yearly	

If you run the same numbers for 15 years, it would be ~ 9.5% and for 20 years, it would be ~ 8%.

While for residential houses, the loan/mortgage period may be approved for 30 years, for commercial loans, the banks are comfortable approving the loan/mortgage only for a period of 15 years maximum. They may approve a loan for 20 years but the revenue stream needs to show a very high level of certainty and consistency.

Even, if you ran the numbers for a 15-year or 20-year scenario, you would find for yourself that the loan amount that you pay in debt service eats up the gross rent completely and you are already in the negative (or in loss). There is nothing more to further calculate or factor in.

List Price	$ 1,800,000.00	
Current Rent	$ 100,000.00	
Cap Rate @ List Price	5.56%	= Rent / List Price
20-year Amortization	$ 114,040.35	Annual Debt Service
Cash remaining	$ (14,040.35)	= Rent - Debt Service

Mind you, this is even before factoring in taxes and expenses. If you were to consider any one of the following or a combination thereof; (1) mortgage periods lower than 15 years, (2) tax brackets higher than 10% and (3) operating expenses, then even after considering deductions and depreciation that may be available to you, it is still only going to make the cash flow run in the negative.

In a 15-year scenario or less, for tax purposes, even if you did deduct the interest portions of your debt service, the difference would not be much and it would continue to drop every month and during the second half of the loan period, the numbers would look a lot worse than what we just ran now.

So, it is clear that if this is how a real estate deal is going to work out for you using a mortgage, then you're better off depositing your money in the banks under CDs which give a maximum rate of 2.5% or even keeping it within your savings account which would give you a maximum rate of 2%.

Now, it may seem better if you run the numbers for a 20-year loan period; a lower mortgage interest rate and a higher than 50% down payment but the simultaneous occurrence of all those events is rare and cannot be used as a rule of thumb. And those people who are a minority within a minority, affording to pay more than 50% down on their rental property purchases, do not need guidance and are truly unaffected by any of the remaining factors.

So, at this point we can conclude that the seller's perspective of fixing a purchase price on commercial properties that would derive a 5-6% cap rate against the rent being currently generated is just plain ludicrous and does not work for the majority of people who are willing to invest in real estate using a mortgage.

Now, many people might still be willing to take up the offer of investment in real estate using a loan/mortgage, especially on the commercial side, even if the cashflow is nearly zero. Why? Keep reading.

Chapter 4

APPRECIATION

This, or maybe 'false' appreciation, is another aspect that both stifles and propels the real estate market at the same time especially in a fantastically stable market like the US. Appreciation is considered to have happened when you buy a property for a certain amount of money and sell it later for a higher amount.

I am not denying the possibility of appreciation. But I am heavily skeptical about people trying to convince me that every area of the country is capable of showing appreciation and more so to a considerable extent.

Of course, there is always the notion that people would rather see 'more' money not realizing that it may have lost value (inflation) than see 'same' amount of money while it retains its value.

Appreciation might be possible for a property when the population in an area is anticipated to grow in the future. The reason is not particularly direct. Increase in crowd traffic leads to increase in demand for the rental space. Increase in demand for rental space means higher rental rates.

<u>In my opinion, it is only when a property is capable of producing higher rent than before, it is deemed to have truly appreciated in value.</u>

Regardless, many buyers would still go into buying a rental property using a loan/mortgage even if it were to produce cashflow at a cap rate less than 1%. And the reason is that they believe that the property will appreciate in value. They believe that they can turn around and sell the property in 1-5 years and derive a lumpsum profit.

This strategy might work but not every time, not everywhere and definitely not to the extent that the buyer would anticipate to profit. In my opinion, it is pure gamble. There is no sensible logic to this kind of blanket investment tactic. It is not universal; it is not absolute and it is not sustainable.

If it is the case that the purchaser bought the property for a fantastic bargain, put in more money to improve the property and then sold it for a considerable lumpsum profit, then <u>that</u> is a reasonable and acceptable strategy.

But I am unable to accept the argument that any property is capable of appreciation only by virtue of passage of time; despite no input on improvement and most importantly, with no increase or even a promise of increase in rental rates. Buyers who purchase properties with only anticipated appreciation to bet on, are only half of the faulty equation.

Most sellers, occupying the other half of the faulty equation, especially in the commercial space, seem to assume that the property has already appreciated since the date of its recent purchase, regardless of the revenue that it is capable of generating. Now, this could be the result of three possibilities. Either (1) they actually honestly believe that such an appreciation has occurred or (2) they have been misled into believing so or (3) they are completely aware that no appreciation has taken place but still continue to overprice the property with the hopes that some ill-informed person would pay an unnecessary premium to purchase it.

Regardless of the reason behind the steep quoting of the list price, the one thing that is certain is that it is unacceptable. Every time a property is purchased for premium price (a price over and above its actual worth), an inflation or bubble is created.

This bubble <u>will</u> burst at some point of time, if the currency retains its value. It may be during the lifetime of the first overpriced purchase or it may be when the third owner down the lane tries to sell it for an even more inflated price. Someone, some day is going to pay the difference!

Examples to demonstrate this theory are plenty and one can see this very often in the residential market. I'm confident that many of you might have read about the 1 billion-dollar property atop the fabulous Beverly Hills that finally sold for a mere $100,000.

The same happened when celebrity 50Cent tried to sell his mansion. Originally, it is said to have been listed for $18.5 million. After 12 long years, it finally sold for only $2.9 million. That was a staggering 84% discount from the original list price.

The same trend can be seen with celebrity Meryl Streep who has recently announced a 26% discount on her NYC penthouse which was originally listed at $24.6 million. The list goes on and on.

While news about residential deals in combination with VIPs hit the media more often, it's very rare or even never that it happens for commercial ones. But the story is always the same. So, we can reasonably infer that it doesn't matter who the seller is or what kind of property is being sold or where the property is located. <u>If a property is overpriced, people will not buy. It will not sell!</u>

These celebrities, VIPs and even regular people pay the price every day for having bought an overpriced property.

Even if they didn't buy it for a premium, they waste valuable time by listing it for a price at which it will never sell. During that time, the property is losing its value (it is becoming an older property), seller is losing money (maintenance, if vacant) and the seller is also losing ROI (return on investment) that he could have derived even if he had invested just half the liquidity of the asset's list price in CDs or stock portfolios, at the very least.

In other words, 50Cent would have gained a lot more if he had sold his mansion for the same $2.9 million, but 12 years earlier.

Chapter 5

REAL PRICE OF A RENTAL PROPERTY

So, we're here after brushing across most factors that could affect or strain your process of purchasing an investment property. So how do we find out the real value of a rental property?

I think the key is in factoring in a loan/mortgage while making this analysis. Because without debt service and operating expenses, any investment that would give a cap rate of 5-7% in the US market, is condonable. Unless involved in real estate or business, it is highly likely that you are paying a sizeable income tax from that cap rate.

Even assuming that the buyer does not need a mortgage and that the list price projects a 5-6% cap rate, it's almost always expected that the buyer would propose a standard bargain to buy the property, which at the very least be a 5-10% discount from the list price.

Assuming that we are working with a range of 5-20% discount, the cap rate may improve to ~ 7.5%. Now, the question is, is this enough?

I had already demonstrated to you that as far as commercial real estate is concerned, the generalized debt service for a period of 15 years would be ~ 9.5% of the loan amount and the loan amount most likely being 80% of the purchase price (which includes closing costs).

Assuming that you got the best discount of 20% on this fantastically overpriced property that is already estimated to give a cap rate of 6%, your cap rate now would be ~ 7.5%. Your debt service alone being ~ 9.5% of the loan amount (80% of purchase price), works out to be 103% of the purchase price! You are losing money and there is nothing else to further calculate when you are already in the negative. See the working below.

List Price	$ 1,800,000.00	
Current Rent	$ 100,000.00	
Cap Rate @ List Price	5.56%	
Modified List Price	$ 1,666,666.67	
Current Rent	$ 100,000.00	
Cap Rate now	6.00%	
20% discounted Price	$ 1,333,333.33	
Cap Rate now	7.50%	
2% Closing Costs added	$ 1,360,000.00	
80% loan amount	$ 1,088,000.00	
Annual Debt service	$ 103,360.00	
Cash in hand	$ (3,360.00)	= Rent - Debt Service

This is even before factoring in operating expenses which you might still have to pay on the property and income taxes which you still have to pay on the $100,000 rent. So, you will be running a deeper negative even after factoring in the depreciation and some basic deductions. Forget breaking even. You will be breaking bad!

To answer the question above, no. A purchase price that gives a 7.5% gross cap rate isn't nearly enough. So, how much is enough?

Let's just tweak the purchase price alone to change the cap rate to 10% and see how that goes. For ease of understanding, the way I have run the numbers is how I would for a person who pretty much has a clean slate. No job, no other business or real estate venture.

The reason is, if you already have a job or a business or few other rental properties or a combination thereof, then you are already paying taxes and the numbers here are only going to be further strained and not relaxed.

However, feel free to modify and run the numbers yourself to best suit your personal financial situation. My numbers, although not wrong, are generalized and made over-simplistic for the purpose of easy and quick understanding about how things basically work.

Modified List Price	$1,000,000.00	
Current Rent	$100,000.00	
Cap Rate now	10.00%	
2% Closing Costs added	$1,020,000.00	
80% loan amount	$816,000.00	
Annual Debt service (DS)	$77,520.00	for 15 years
Cash remaining (Rent - DS)	$22,480.00	Before taxes and expenses
Value of building	$800,000.00	Assumed to be 80% of purchase price. Could be more or less.
Depreciation (Commercial)	$20,253.16	Value of building divided by 39.5 (number of years)
Standard Deduction	$24,000.00	Assuming you are married and this is the first and only source of income
Operating Expenses	$10,000.00	Assuming it is only 10% of gross income
Taxable Income	$45,746.84	= Rent - Depreciation - Deduction - Op Exp
Tax @ 10%	$4,574.68	
Net Income (Annual)	$7,905.32	= Cash remaining - Op exp - tax
Net Income (Monthly)	$658.78	
Net Cap Rate	0.78%	on last payment of DS
	1.16%	on first payment of DS

As you can see, with a gross cap rate of 10%, the net cap rate is ~ 0.8% on the last payment of your debt service and ~ 1.2% on the first. This change happens because only the interest portion of your debt service are deductible against the taxable income.

Since amortized, the interest portion continues to reduce every month, thus giving rise to change in the net cap rate. This gives an average net cap rate of ~ 1%. This is still less than the ~2.5% gross offered by CDs in banks, right?

Let us tweak the value a little more. Let us see what we get with a 12% cap rate.

Modified List Price	$	833,333.33	
Current Rent	$	100,000.00	
Cap Rate now		12.00%	
2% Closing Costs added	$	850,000.00	
80% loan amount	$	680,000.00	
Annual Debt service (DS)	$	64,600.00	for 15 years
Cash remaining (Rent - DS)	$	35,400.00	Before taxes and expenses
Value of building	$	666,666.67	Assumed to be 80% of purchase price. Could be more or less.
Depreciation (Commercial)	$	16,877.64	Value of building divided by 39.5 (number of years)
Standard Deduction	$	24,000.00	Assuming you are married and this is the first and only source of income
Operating Expenses	$	10,000.00	Assuming it is only 10% of gross income
Taxable Income	$	49,122.36	= Rent - Depreciation - Deduction - Op Exp
Tax @ 10%	$	4,912.24	
Net Income (Annual)	$	20,487.76	= Cash remaining - Op exp - tax
Net Income (Monthly)	$	1,707.31	
Net Cap Rate		2.41%	on last payment of DS
		2.79%	on first payment of DS

Now, you can see that with a gross cap rate of 12%, the net cap rate is ~ 2.8% on the first payment of your debt service and ~ 2.4% on the last. The average net cap is ~ 2.6%. It is only at this point that the numbers begin to make sense and provide returns that are worth the risk and effort involved. And it is net income. So, this is just enough.

So, we can reasonably infer that when using a loan/mortgage, a property that generates a cap rate less than 12% is not worth pursuing. Of course, all the variables mentioned above such as, length of loan period, percentage of down payment, interest on loan amount, applicable taxes, deductions, depreciation, etc., could all change from property to property and from person to person. You should make changes accordingly and run the numbers to see what works and does not work for you.

If you need a general, simple and quick guide to figuring out the best price for a rental property, just remember the following.

In my opinion, as of 2019, **the real price of a rental property, especially in the commercial sector, is only anywhere between 8 to 12 times the rent that the property generates or is capable of reasonably generating.**

For example, if a commercial rental property is currently generating $75,000 annually at full occupancy. Then the true value of the property is anywhere between $600,000 (75,000 x 8) and $900,000 (75,000 x 12). The same approach with reasonable modifications can be applied to residential properties, as well.

But where the price falls within this range depends on the kind of property (residential or commercial), location of the site, quality of the infrastructure, potential vacancy/occupancy rate and most importantly, the financial situation of the person making the offer to buy.

In my opinion, <u>any price that is less than 8 times the rent is a steal; and any price that is more than 12 times the rent is premium</u>.

Now that you have been informed, get out there and make offers confidently knowing that you are not wrong. Sure, it might take a while for the market to acknowledge this fact. But only when more and more people make the same kind of sensible offers and stick to them, will the sector get reformed and allow the market to be more fluid and vibrant with trades occurring all the time.

-x-x-x-

www.ingramcontent.com/pod-product-compliance
Lightning Source LLC
Chambersburg PA
CBHW070906220526
45466CB00005B/2146